Kaleidoscope

Delfina Serra

BookLeaf
Publishing

India | USA | UK

Presentation by *BookLeaf Publishing*

Web: www.bookleafpub.com

E-mail: info@bookleafpub.com

ISBN: 9789358316599

First edition 2024

DEDICATION

I dedicate this book to my children and my husband, who have supported me throughout my life. A special dedication to my mother, who has always believed in me and asked that I would one day write a book.

ACKNOWLEDGEMENT

I want to dedicate a special thank you to my youngest child, Zezito, who has helped me in writing and curating/facilitating the creation of this book.

PREFACE

I'm writing this message for my mother, and for all those who have the opportunity to read her work. My mum has given me everything I need from this life. She is the light that guides me every day, and the warmth that hugs me throughout my every challenge.

I could write a million words about my mum and they would never be enough. Delfina. You deserve to have your dreams come true, and it's my privilege to help you take one step closer.

Obrigado por tudo que tu fazes por nós, Mãe Gosto muito de ti.

Beyond Reason

When I'm no longer here
When I no longer hear you calling

Don't cry for me

Because I am not a memory
Or a picture on the wall

Stop!

Sit down

Because I am the sun
That warms you in winter

The breeze
That refreshes your summer

I am this love
That you carry in your heart

I am the affection
That you carry in your eyes

I was her

Who loved you,

Beyond reason

A Little Place

I have a little place
Where I hide all of my pain

It only belongs to me
I don't show it to anyone else

That pain
Contains all my love as well

All my smiles
My embrace
My memories

I keep in that little place

Within my chest
It lives inside my heart

I will keep it that way
Until that day arrives

Where I may pass away
And meet you again

The Flowers in My Garden

My garden has flowers
In my home, joy is king
My heart contains lovers
That fill me with vanity

The flowers in my garden
Dance at the taste of wind
They are everything to me
The ones that give me breath

I water my flowers with kindness,
With love and dedication
And I tell them, quietly:
 "You live within my heart"

A heart much stronger
At the sight of watching you grow
You are my everything
My direction, my north
Forward
I will love you beyond dusk

My children

The Little Boy

The little boy cried
Without love or bread
He looked to everyone
With no one to call brother

The little boy cried
Without knowing who gave him life
He looked to everyone
With no place to call home

The little boy cried
Without understanding
Why no one loved him
He wanted to know

But somebody found him
Sheltered and showed him love
He never cried once more
Finally having someone to call mother

Wings to Imagination

I thought of travelling
Escaping without reason
I found myself at sea
So full of emotion

I found myself thinking
How would I live without you?
If it is loving you so
That life has reason to me

In that wave of feelings
In that love so enormous
Where you can hear my sorrow
And my heart goes to sleep

I won't travel
Run away, I can't either
Come to me!
Let's love each other
Giving wings to imagination

Forever, I Will Love You

I dreamt of your embrace
I felt your heart beating
Anxious for your grasp
I long to see you once more

You left without warning
And I wasn't prepared
Forever,
I will love you
And await your return

You won't come back!
I know it!

But one day,
I will find you again
With patience I will await
To embrace you once more

For my Father

No Direction

I went from door to door
I begged for love
I dragged myself upon the floor
No one saw my suffering

I cried tears of solitude
With nothing to grasp onto
No one to offer their hand
No one to love

In this world,
I am alone
Sad and abandoned
I pity myself
Offering love with nothing in return

For a family, a home
Someone to give me shelter
I have so much love to give
I walk this earth with no direction

You Never Saw Me

I spoke of myself,
For myself
What was and what happened
Where it was that I lost myself
Feeling a love that wasn't mine

Why did I pursue you?
When you already loved her
I didn't know what else to do
Because you never once saw me

This feeling,
Imprudent
Irresponsible and without reason
It corrodes within
It tastes of betrayal

All that I want is to have you
So what if you're not mine
But I still await you
That one day you tell me
That your love for her died

Fervour

When you arrived I was naked
And I wasn't embarrassed
You know that I'm yours
I never denied it

For you,
With modesty,
I unravel
And dress myself in passion

You are the reason I exist
The reason my heart beats

You are my world
But I'm only a lover to you
My most profound wish
Is to have you only to myself

I know you have another love
But your body searches for mine
I am the only one that brings you that fervour
Only I,
bring you that madness

Empty

Disentangled!
I had nothing

I loved!
Unrequited

I searched!
You were nowhere to be found

I cried!
But you never dropped a tear

I screamed!
Silence took over

I made you the breath from my lungs
I created an illusion
I had so much to give you
Never recognising the reason

With myself at the forefront
I ravelled myself in golden wrapping
Pretending I didn't see
That you did not want me by your side

You were pale of love
Of empty feeling
Your world had no colour
You were cruel and cold

Who I Always Wanted

Only you were who I always wanted
My most precious passion
My fantasy
Your hand would never open to me

For you,
I lost everything
But you were the one,
Who betrayed me
Who played me
Who left me abandoned

And still I say
Only you were who I always wanted
You were my night
You were my day

For You

I awoke in the morning
And looked at my flowers in the garden
In this dewy morning
You already smiled to me

You arrived early
With that glow
That love from which I drink
That path of which I tread
The path of perdition

When I open the window for you
And we live in that passion
In all the fire within it

When you enter my room
And I would undress my values
For you,
I am thirsty
For you,
I am lost

And within those burning bodies
We unite with fervour
In my house
We make love

My Purpose

It was I!
Who put you on this earth

It was I!
Who dried your first tears

It was I!
Who held your hand in your first steps

It was I!
Who heard your first words

It is I!
Who always smiles alongside your conquests

It is I!
Who suffers when you weep

It is I!
Who will always await you

It is I!
Who love you until your last breath

Where Are You?

I walked over my feelings
Between valleys and hills

Cried rivers of tears
And yet you didn't come
To comfort my fears

You don't want my love
But for you
I fly down and above

That Woman

I watched myself in the mirror
There was someone else in my place
I was surprised
Not finding myself

I had wrinkles and white hair
And I was watching myself
To my astonishment
I was actually enjoying it

I was also wiser
And I invited myself to accept
I didn't want to follow her lips
But I was actually enjoying it

Then I noticed!
There were similarities
Was it really me?...

But I was no longer a child
And so I accepted
It was that woman
That I became

My Everything

I looked back
Couldn't find myself
Without you

I just survived
Like an ornament
A book on a shelf

Where are you?
Come to me!

This is a torment
You are my breath
My sunshine
For our love,
I live

I'm yours
You are mine

What You Can See

You don't know me
I'm not a smile
Not a body
But a soul

I swallow my tears
Hiding my fears
Yes!

You don't know me
I hide inside this shell
Because what matters is what you can see

I am sorrow
Cruelty
But what matters is what you can see

That smile that I borrow
The love that I pretend

You don't know me
In the end

What matters is what you can see

Left Behind

I kissed you...
Turned my back,
Ignored our farewell

You tell me that you like it
But I see
That you live with a wounded soul

The visit comes to an end
The hour is calling
Something shatters within me
In your eyes, I see a tear
Withheld and unshed

You call her, home
But I know that you lie
With so much love for me

You don't say how you feel
I wish I could embrace you
I wish I could bring you back

But I also cannot,
I need to leave you be
Where you now call,
A home

Lend Me Your Hand

I left without knowing
I still wanted you
I lost you in the chase
To someone who didn't deserve you
Loved
Suffered
I have cried and I have fallen
Looking back
Noticing
Everything I had lost
I was blind and I ignored
Everything we had together
How much I hurt you
The blame was only mine

I ask for forgiveness
Return to me, please
Lend me your hand
Remember our love

Our Garden

My garden has flowers
Yours is empty
In my heart, lovers exist
In yours, only shadows and cold

My garden has a little bird
Yours is empty
He wants to build his nest
But yours
Accepts no one

There is sunshine in my garden
Yours, filled with darkness
You should nurture jasmine
And open your heart

If you returned to my garden
I would share the sun with you
If you looked at me once more
Maybe, you would love me some day

You Will Remember, Tomorrow

An old lady cried
Lost and abandoned
Because the ones who she loved
Would no longer visit for anything

Once before, she would have company
A house stacked with others
But now she suffers
Watching herself, alone and depressed

Everyone went away
They searched for their future
Forgetting now,
Who gave them a love so pure

But if a son you are,
A father you will become
And what you do today
You will remember, tomorrow